Kid's Word Cookbook
BOOK 3

Scott Ravede

Copyright 2023 | Scott Ravede

ISBN: 978-1-7348671-7-6 (case-laminate)
            978-1-7348671-8-3 (paperback)
            978-1-7348671-9-0 (epub)

All rights reserved.

Printed in the USA.

No part of this book may be copied or reproduced in any form or manner without the expressed written permission of the author and publisher.

Scott Ravede Books
Scott@ScottRavedeBooks.com
www.ScottRavedeBooks.com

Disclaimer: Eating your words is a figure of speech and not meant to be taken literally, and following the recipes in this book will not actually result in edible food.

Special Note: Check out the "wordy" recipes in this book, so you can see how these dishes were made. But, kids, please don't touch the kitchen utensils without your parent's permission.

Illustrated by Rivka Ravede, rivkaravede73@gmail.com

Welcome to the Kid's Word Cookbook Series

Since American English is a melting pot of words from multiple cultures, learning it can be confusing. So, what to do with this "melting pot of words?" Why, cook them, of course! The Kid's Word Cookbook Series brings some levity to the situation by using a combination of silly stories and artwork to help students learn some popular elements of our language. (And to help everyone else just to have some fun).

This book contains five silly stories, each ending with a whimsical recipe where the reader is cooking up words instead of food.

The elements of language used throughout the book are defined in the glossary.

The words related to the elements of language used in each story appear as a list of ingredients in the recipes.

The particular language elements themselves will be in the recipe directions.

A note to teachers and parents: The books ascend in level of sophistication as you progress through the series. So, beginning readers will want to start with Book 1 and go in order. Expert readers can ignore this advice and go in any order they choose.

GLOSSARY

Alliteration: repetition of the first consonant sound in 2 or more words close together.
Example: Crazy kids kicked cans on the corner in Colorado. (repetition of hard "c" sound)

Assonance: repetition of vowel sounds in non-rhyming stressed syllables.
Example: No one knows the road home. (repetition of long "o" sound)

Circular Reasoning: occurs when the end of an argument comes back to the beginning without having proven itself.
Example: I am wise. How do I know I am wise? Because I am wise.

Consonance: repetition of the same consonant sound anywhere in the word in 2 or more words close together.
Example: Get the egg and don't forget. (repetition of hard "g" sound)

Heteronyms: words that are spelled the same but have different pronunciations and meanings.
Example: lead (what a leader does) and lead (the heavy metal)

Homonyms: words that are pronounced and spelled the same but have different meanings.
Example: bark (part of a tree) and bark (what a noisy dog does)

Homophones: words that are pronounced the same, may or may not be spelled the same, but have different meanings.

Example: flower and flour

Near Homophones: words that are pronounced almost the same, may or may not be spelled the same, and have different meanings.

Example: loose and lose

Heterographs: words that are pronounced the same but have different spellings and meanings.

Example: sun and son

Homographs: words that are spelled the same, may or may not be pronounced the same, but have different meanings.

Example: bow (bend at the waist), bow (knotted ribbon) and bow (front of a boat)

Mondegreens: words or phrases resulting from a mishearing of other words or phrases.

Example: hearing "dude day" for "today" or "tomb arrow" for "tomorrow"

Oronyms: different words or phrases that sound the same.

Example: "I love you" and "Isle of Hugh"

GLOSSARY

Reverse Oronyms: 2 sets of words or phrases in which each set is the oronym of the other in reverse word order.

Example: "a lone" and "loan a"

Rhymes: words that have the same ending sound.

Example: take and make

- **Identical Rhymes:** rhyming of words with the same words.

    Example: wear and wear

- **Imperfect Rhymes:** words that come close to rhyming but don't exactly rhyme.

    Example: from and prom

- **Masculine Rhymes:** rhyming of only one syllable, the stressed and final syllable.

    Example: aside and reside

- **Rich Rhymes:** rhyming syllables or words that sound identical or are homophones.

    Example: wear and where

- **Unstressed Rhymes:** rhyming of unstressed syllables.

    Example: seaside and beachside

Kid's Word Cookbook
BOOK 3

It should be a piece of cake
when it's words you bake.
But mark my word,
you'll eat your words,
when you're in the thick of the war
between Ward and Ward's ward.

There are hares here,
and hairs and ears here,
and recipes that you can
cook up with a toucan.
Check them out at the end of each dish.
You will enjoy them. They are delish!

Too Many Toucans

One needs cans when shopping for toucans.
If one can get one toucan in one can
then one can get one toucan.

Too Many Toucans

If one buys more than one toucan,
one can use two cans.
If one's toucans don't fit in two cans
one can use more than two cans
for one's toucans.

Too Many Toucans

More than two cans should be more than enough for one's toucans
when one's toucans number more than two toucans.

Too Many Toucans

You too can have a toucan
if you have one can.
And if you have two cans
you too can have two toucans.

Too Many Toucans

And if you have more than two cans
you too can have more than two toucans—
unless more than two toucans are too many toucans.

Too Many Toucans

You may need more than one can
for one toucan doing the cancan.
And if the toucan is in a tutu
you will need at least two.

Too Many Toucans

And if the toucan in the tutu is doing the cancan
you will need a special tutu-cancan-toucan can.

Too Many Toucans

And what about two toucans in two tutus doing two cancans?
For that you will need two tutu-cancan-toucan cans.

Too Many Toucans

And if you have more than two toucans
in more than two tutus doing more than two cancans?
Well, that's just too many tutu-wearing cancan-dancing toucans.

RECIPE

Too Many Toucans

INGREDIENTS

one	toucan	two	too can
can	toucans	two cans	cancan
cans	one can	two toucans	tutu

LANGUAGE ELEMENTS

Homonyms	Oronyms	Rich Rhymes	Alliteration
Homophones	Consonance	Identical Rhymes	

DIRECTIONS

In a gruel of homonyms, homophones, rich rhymes,
identical rhymes and alliteration
cook one, can, one can, toucan and cancan
in one consonance can if you can, with one toucan.
Or if you have two cans,
cook two, cans, toucans, two cans, two toucans, too can and tutu
in two oronyms cans
while dancing the cancan in a tutu with two toucans in two tutus.
One can do this two times if not too tired.

Left Leaves

While a wind blows the leaves,
leaving no leaves on the trees,
you'd say the leaves have been leaving,
before the leaves have all left.

Left Leaves

If a left-leaning tree
has only leaves on the left,
will the tree go upright
when the leaves have all left?

Left Leaves

Leif lifts a leaf off the right and a leaf off the left,
until there's only one leaf left,
neither to the right nor the left.
But if there are no leaves to the right,
can there be a leaf that is left?

RECIPE

Left Leaves

INGREDIENTS

leaves   left   leaf
leaving   Leif

LANGUAGE ELEMENTS

Homonyms   Assonance
Alliteration   Homophones

DIRECTIONS

Butter a thick piece of alliteration bread
with leaves, leaving and Leif on the left,
homonyms, homophones and assonance on the right,
leaving leaf and left off
and then leave when done reading
if you are still upright.

Moos, Moose and Muumuus

For a cow to be heard, it has to moo.
In order to moo, it has to be in the mood.

Moos, Moose and Muumuus

Once a cow has mooed
it will stay in the mood to moo,
and will moo at anything that wanders through,
including a moose in a muumuu that is too mute to moo.

Moos, Moose and Muumuus

When a moose moos at the moon and a cow moos at it too,
the moose moos will be muted by the more moosy cow moos,
making the point of the moose moos as moot as moose muumuus.

RECIPE

Moos, Moose and Muumuus

INGREDIENTS

mood   moose
mooed   moos

LANGUAGE ELEMENTS

Homophones   Assonance   Heterographs
Near Homophones   Alliteration

DIRECTIONS

When you're in the mood,
place mood, mooed, moose and moos in the center of a pan buttered with
homophones, near homophones, assonance, alliteration and heterographs
and bake until the cows come home.
Wait until the moose have mooed before reading.

The Hares Here

Here is a hare.

Here is a hair.

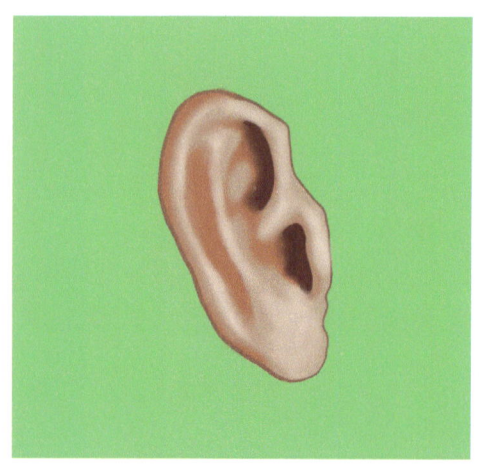

Here is an ear.

Here is an heir.

The Hares Here

Here is a hare
with hair in its ear.

Here is a hare
with air in its ear.

Here is a hare
with air in its hair.

Here is a hare
with an heir in its hair.

Here is a hare
with air in its hair
and air in its ear.

The Hares Here

Hairy hares have many hairs.
That's what makes them hairy hares.

The Hares Here

Hairy hares hop from here to there.
Hairy hares hop from ear to ear.
Hairy hares always hop back here,
when they are all out of air
from hopping here to ear.

The Hares Here

The hares here will be up to their ears in heirs
when the heirs of the hares get here.
But you will not hear when the heirs get here,
if you are a hare with hair in your ear.

The Hares Here

Hairy hares with hair on their ears
leave hair to their heirs.
When their heirs get here, they get the hair
as the heirs to the hares with hair on their ears.
But if the heirs of the hares put on airs when they're here,
then air is all they'll leave with from here.

RECIPE

The Hares Here

INGREDIENTS

hare	hear	air	heirs
here	ear	hares	airs
hair	heir	hairs	

LANGUAGE ELEMENTS

Alliteration	Near Homophones	Identical Rhymes
Assonance	Heterographs	Imperfect Rhymes
Homophones	Rich Rhymes	

DIRECTIONS

Put whatever you have here in a large mixing bowl with plenty of air and mix in here, hear, ear, heir, heirs, and airs.

Beat with alliteration until you hear the heir tell you to stop.

(If you don't hear anything, get the hair out of your ears.)

Add hare, hair, air, hares and hairs

and blend in assonance, homophones and near homophones.

Top off with a garnish of rich rhymes, identical rhymes and imperfect rhymes.

Serves 8 heirs as long as they're not putting on airs.

The War Between Ward and His Ward

Ward warred with his ward in Ware,
when his ward in Ware
dared to wear
Ward's unworn underwear.

The War Between Ward and His Ward

Worn out from war,
Ward's ward gave his word to Ward,
to award Ward more underwear,
for Ward ending the war.

The War Between Ward and His Ward

True to his word,
Ward's war-weary ward
warred no more with Ward,
and awarded Ward more underwear
when Ward ended the war.

The War Between Ward and His Ward

Ward's ward was rewarded for keeping his word,
with an award from Ward.
And nothing about that award was untoward,
unlike the underwear that Ward's ward took from Ward.

RECIPE

The War Between Ward and His Ward

INGREDIENTS

Ward	Ware	word	rewarded
warred	wear	award	untoward
ward	war	awarded	

LANGUAGE ELEMENTS

Identical Rhymes	Alliteration	Near Homophones	Homonyms
Assonance	Homophones	Heterographs	Masculine Rhymes

DIRECTIONS

Wear your apron while making a paste out of
Ward, warred, ward, Ware, wear, war and word.
Knead into a dough or until you are worn out.
Cover dough thoroughly with
identical rhymes, masculine rhymes, assonance, alliteration, homophones,
near homophones, heterographs and homonyms
and cut into strips of award, awarded, rewarded and untoward.
Bake for 20 minutes.
The word around Ware is that you will be rewarded for your efforts.

Questions for *Kid's Word Cookbook: Book 3*

1. Is a can the best thing for carrying a toucan?

2. Is there a store in your town that sells toucans?

3. Have you ever seen a toucan in a tutu? How about a toucan doing the cancan?

4. What's the difference between a regular toucan can and a tutu-cancan-toucan can?

5. How many toucans is too many toucans?

6. Have you ever seen the wind blow all the leaves off a tree?

7. Have you ever seen a tree with only leaves on the left? Or the right?

8. If there is only one leaf on a tree, can it be to the right or the left of any other leaves?

9. What's the plural of moose?

10. Which moos louder, a moose or a cow?

11. Does a moose even moo?

12. Would a muumuu look good on a moose? Or would it be better on a cow?

13. Are hares hairy? Are there any hares that aren't hairy?

14. Would you be able to hear if you had hair in your ear?
    Or if you had air in your ear?

15. Would you want to be an heir to a hare?

16. Should Ward have warred with his ward over underwear?

17. Why didn't Ward's ward return the underwear he took?

18. Did you like the award that Ward's ward got Ward?

I hope you enjoyed the book.

Please send any comments, questions, or suggestions to

Scott@ScottRavedeBooks.com.

I would greatly appreciate any review you would care to leave at online booksellers.

I look forward to exploring the flavor of words with you in my next book.

Cheers!

Scott Ravede

Ordering Information

To order additional copes of this book, find out more about Scott Ravede, or get a heads-up on his new books, visit www.ScottRavedeBooks.com.

You can also email the author at Scott@ScottRavedeBooks.com.

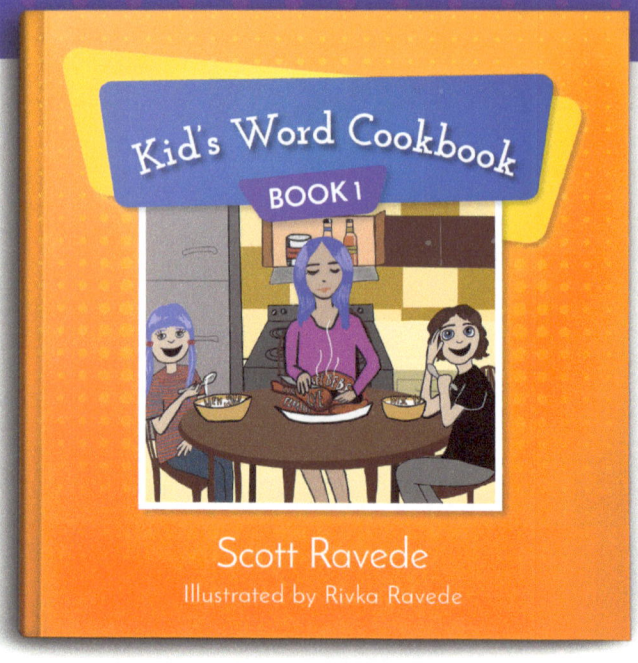

Get ready to eat your words.
Regular food is for the birds.
Don't be a dummy.
Forget about your tummy.

Pay attention to your vocal cords,
and get gorging on some lo-cal words.
By digging into these fine recipes,
you'll have more fun
than the flies and the fleas.

ScottRavedeBooks.com

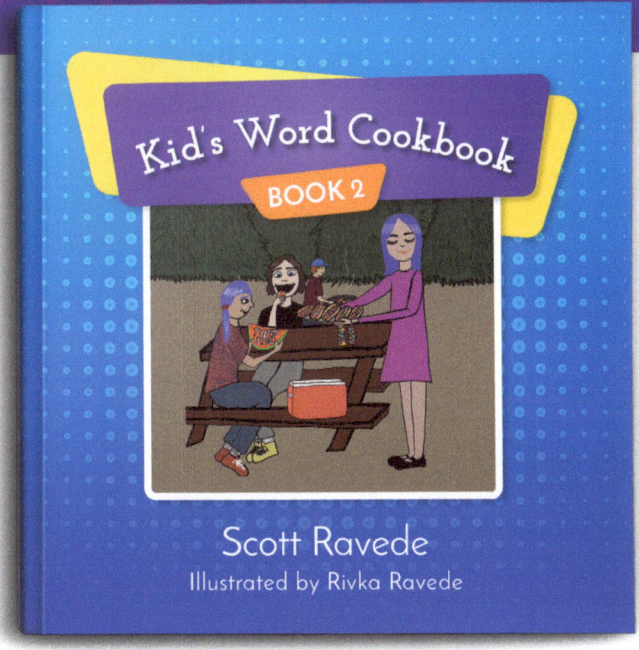

Hot dog, hot dog,
the second book is here!
The hot dogs here are not what they appear.
Hot off the grill, they give your mouth a thrill.
It's not meat you eat, but rather a wordy treat.

Be sure to savor the can and can't bees,
but not before trying the ties and the tees.
You will find the recipes at the end of each dish,
but if you're a good word chef,
skip them, if you wish.

ScottRavedeBooks.com

www.ingramcontent.com/pod-product-compliance
Lightning Source LLC
Chambersburg PA
CBHW040728150426
42811CB00063B/1541